In loving memory of
the Princess who never became queen
and Rowdy,
who would have been her consort
as well as a budgie named Tiki.

First published in 2021 by Panoma Press Ltd .

This edition published by Markosia Enterprises, Ltd, January 2024.
Harry Markos, Director.
www.markosia.com

Illustrations by Nilesh B. Mistry
Book layout by Nilesh B. Mistry, Mainline Design Limited.

Hardback: ISBN 978-1-916968-12-7
eBook: ISBN 978-1-916968-13-4

For Markosia Enterpises Ltd:

Harry Markos
Publisher & Managing Partner

GM Jordan
Special Projects Co-Ordinator

Andy Briggs
Creative Consultant

Ian Sharman
Editor In Chief

The Sphinxing Rabbit

Les Très Riches Heures du Duc de Bunny

Written by Pauline Chakmakjian
Illustrated by Nilesh Mistry

The Sphinxing Rabbit became bored with society due to its dumbing down.

4

After all her efforts to create a
prosperous society of learning,
sloth took over.

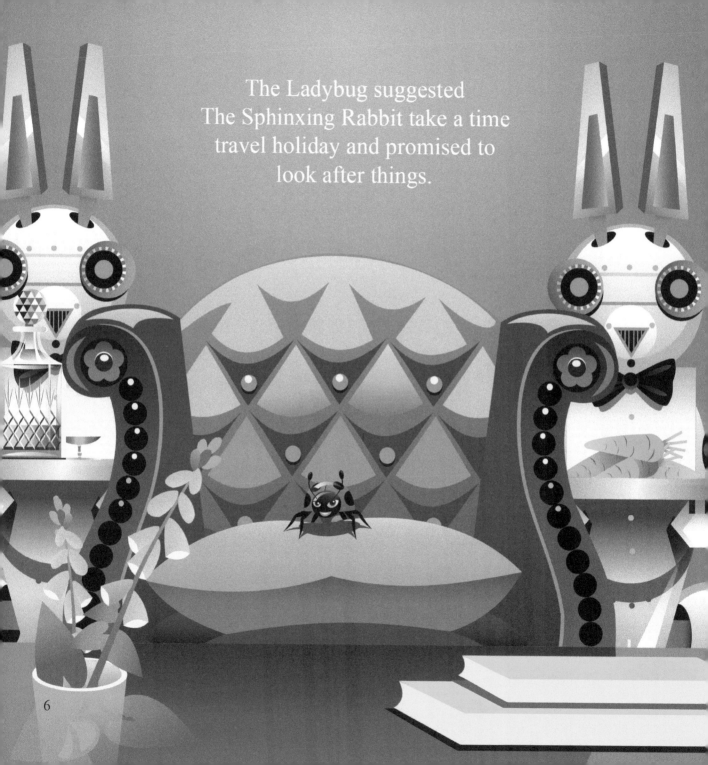

The Ladybug suggested
The Sphinxing Rabbit take a time
travel holiday and promised to
look after things.

6

The Sphinxing Rabbit used the time
machine to travel to Medieval Europe
and packed accordingly.

She first visited dear friends she
hadn't seen for a long while.

And then took a rest in
a peaceful, enchanted
forest to the sound of
chirping birds.

9

The Duc de Bunny sees
The Sphinxing Rabbit while
riding in the forest.

She is blissfully asleep now.

He has one of his courtiers place a
most perfect bunch of carrots for
her as a gift.

The birds stopped chirping so
The Sphinxing Rabbit was awakened.
She looked carefully around before
tasting the carrots.

"Ahem! Do you like the carrots?"

"Yes, indeed, I do, thank you."

"They are the best I could procure from my
lands for I am the Duc de –"

"Bunny, yes, I know."

"But, how? I have never seen you before
in my domain."

"I'm from the future and the Duc de Bunny
is in the blockchain of archival information
under my domain name."

"I say, what ever is a blockchain?
Please be my guest and tell me all about it."

The Sphinxing Rabbit and the Duc de Bunny
rode to the Duke's chateau.

The Duke listened to
The Sphinxing Rabbit attentively
for several hours with great interest.

22

The Sphinxing Rabbit explained
everything about mutual
distributed ledgers over supper.

23

"Oh, I see, how delightfully fascinating.
But, I am a bit perplexed by peer-to-peer.
Anyway, tomorrow we shall ride out so
I can show you some of my lands."

24

The next day, The Sphinxing Rabbit
encountered some of the peasants
on the Duke's land.

"You see I don't have peers here,
only serfs."

28

The Sphinxing Rabbit asked
the Duke why the serfs looked
the way they do.

The Duke replied, "I do believe it is because they have the poor gene. We don't since we are a fancy breed of rabbit."

"Poor gene? Don't be ridiculous! They can be educated and operate using blockchain just as we can."

"Hmmm, I say, is that not rather dangerous? I mean, how would one ever get them to do any work?"

32

"Force shouldn't be used,
but persuasion like I did."

"Mmmm, I suppose you are right, but they can neither read nor write. Might I simply lavish them with entertainments, a joust perhaps and a sumptuous banquet, and they can just place their mark on some parchment agreeing to do whatever I propose?"

34

"Well, I suppose that is one idea, but it would rather be better for them to be educated properly in order to truly appreciate your proposals and then decide whether they agree to them."

The Duke had a special academy built by his
masons according to specifications given by
The Sphinxing Rabbit.

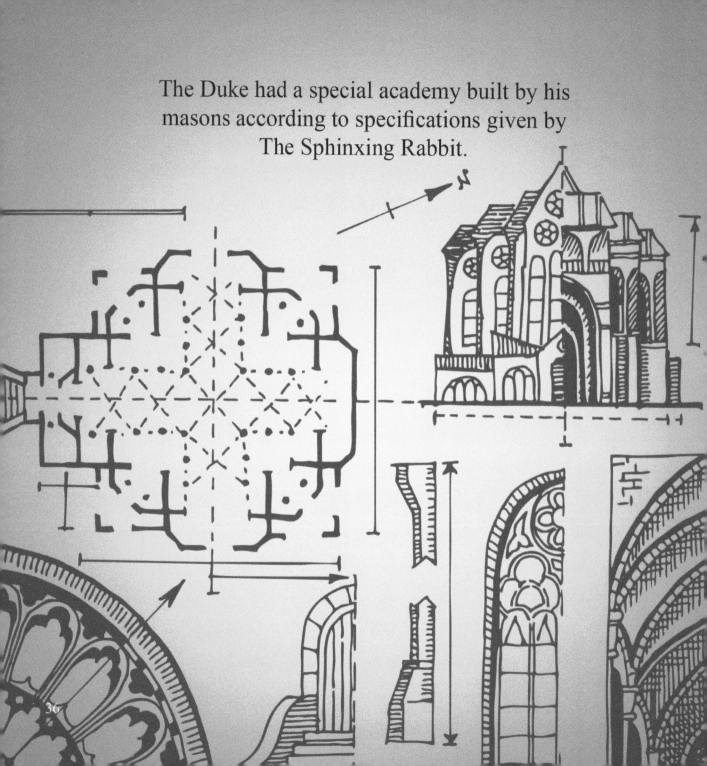

Some months passed as the serfs received knowledge to become peers – nearly all were transformed.

Developers, engineers and other various types
of talented individuals emerged.

But alas, let's face it, not *everyone*
could be helped.

The Duke described how technology
is the way forward and the people
understood and agreed.

The Duc de Bunny also commissioned a charming Book of Hours for several, possible blockchain applications using smart ledgers.

42 January – Identity, Birth Certificates and Genealogical Trees

February – Vehicle Registries

March – Land and Property Titles

April – Tracking of Diamond Features

May – Provenance of Artwork

June – Recording of Cultural Events 47

48   July – Qualifications and Degrees

August – Music Ownership and Payment Transparency 49

September – Shipping Registries

October – Trading Records

November – Archiving Historical Events

December – Criminal, Court and Death Records

The Duke gave a special copy
to The Sphinxing Rabbit
in appreciation for all the
organizational changes she
had helped to bring about
to his fiefdom.

54

The Sphinxing Rabbit thanked the
Duc de Bunny for his hospitality, generosity
and open-mindedness to reforms.

Meeting in the middle, they agreed neo-feudalism would
be a jolly way forward for society.

But, they may be branded as tyrannical so it was thought best
to conceal this with a veneer of democracy.

The Duc de Bunny asked what
it was like living in the time of
The Sphinxing Rabbit.

The Sphinxing Rabbit suggested
they return to the present so he could
see her warren.

"Oh, how disconcerting, I much prefer
my fiefdom!"

61

To be continued…

Special thanks to
my father,
Dr. George Chakmakjian

Author

Pauline Chakmakjian is an author,
artist, public speaker, advisor
and a Freeman of the City of London.

Illustrator

Milesh Mistry is an illustrator,
designer and mural artist.
www.nileshmistry.com